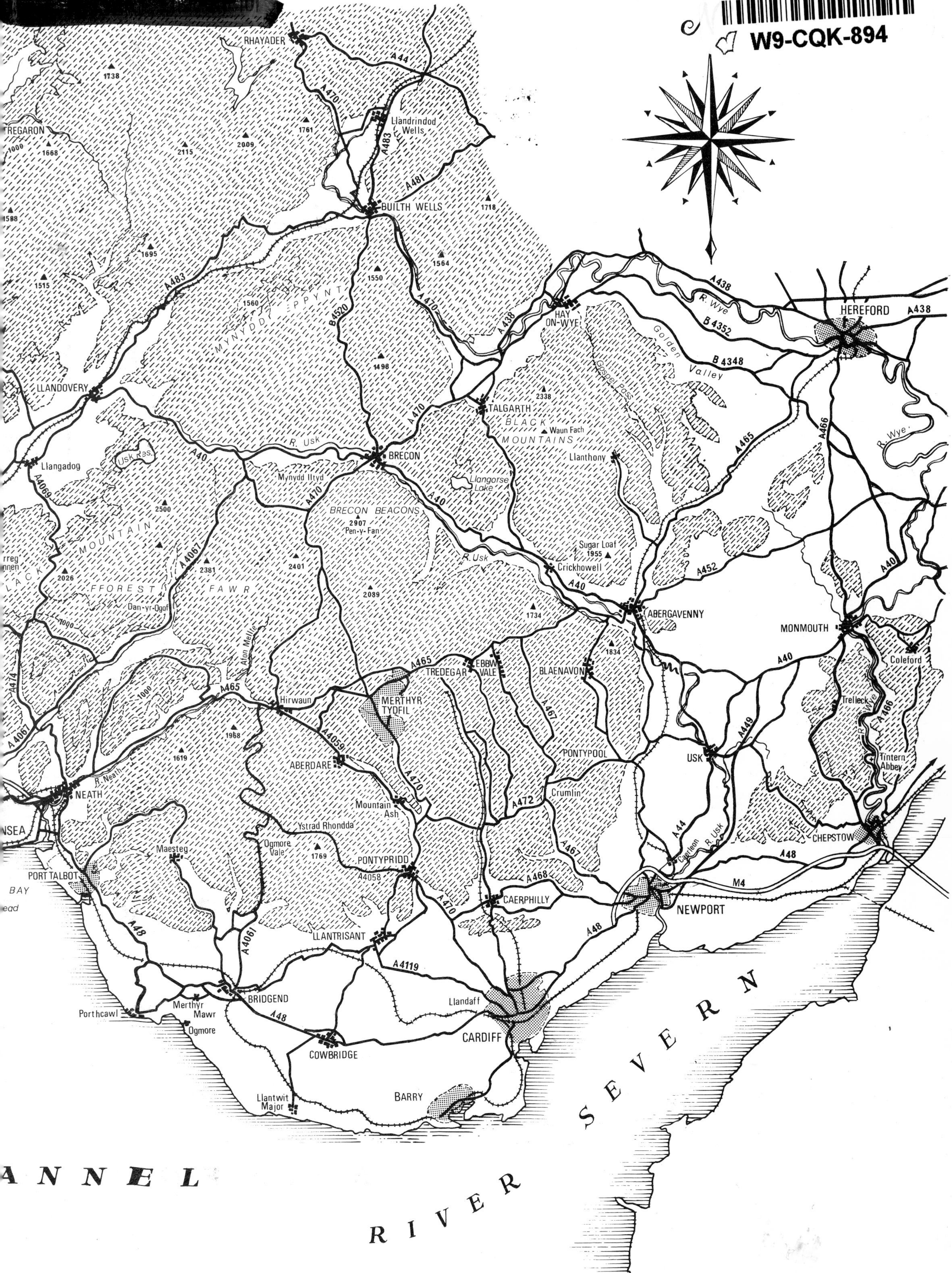
RHAYADER
1738
A44
A470
Llandrindod
Wells
1761
TREGARON
1000
1668
2115
2009
A483
A481
BUILTH WELLS
1718
1588
1695
1564
1515
1550
A483
1560
MYNYDD EPPYNT
B4520
A470
A438
HAY
ON-WYE
R. Wye
A438
HEREFORD
A438
B 4352
Golden
Valley
B 4348
1498
LLANDOVERY
TALGARTH
2338
BLACK
MOUNTAINS
Waun Fach
Gospel Pass
A466
R. Wye
A465
R. Usk
Usk Res.
A40
BRECON
Llanthony
Llangadog
Mynydd Illtyd
Llangorse
Lake
A4069
A470
A40
BRECON BEACONS
2907
Pen-y-Fan
2500
MOUNTAIN
Sugar Loaf
1955
R. Usk
Crickhowell
A452
A40
A4067
2401
2381
2026
FFOREST
FAWR
2089
A40
Dan-yr-Ogof
1734
ABERGAVENNY
MONMOUTH
1000
Afon Mellte
1834
Coleford
A465
TREDEGAR
EBBW
VALE
BLAENAVON
A40
A474
1000
A465
Hirwaun
MERTHYR
TYDFIL
A467
Trelleck
R. Wye
A466
A4061
1968
A4059
A449
1619
ABERDARE
PONTYPOOL
USK
Tintern
Abbey
R. Neath
NEATH
A470
Crumlin
A472
Mountain
Ash
Ystrad Rhondda
A44
R. Usk
Caerleon
CHEPSTOW
Maesteg
Ogmore
Vale
1769
PONTYPRIDD
A467
A48
PORT TALBOT
BAY
A4058
A468
M4
CAERPHILLY
NEWPORT
A48
A4061
A470
LLANTRISANT
A48
A4119
BRIDGEND
Llandaff
Merthyr
Mawr
Porthcawl
A48
Ogmore
CARDIFF
COWBRIDGE
Llantwit
Major
BARRY
SEVERN
ANNEL
RIVER

South Wales
in cameracolour

South Wales
in cameracolour

TEXT AND PHOTOGRAPHS BY DEREK FORSS

914.294

Town & County
BOOKS
LONDON

A member of the Ian Allan Group

2/7/93   43T

Bibliography

Portrait of South Wales, Michael Senior, Robert Hale, 1974

South Wales, Ruth Thomas, Bartholomew, 1977

A South Wales Sketchbook, A. Wainwright, Westmorland Gazette, 1983

Wales, Wynford Vaughan Thomas, Michael Joseph, 1981

The Big Walks & Classic Walks — Sections on walking in Pembrokeshire, Brecon Beacons and Black Mountains, various authors, Diadem Books, 1980 & 1982

Through Welsh Border Country following Offa's Dyke Path, Mark Richards, Thornhill Press, 1976

Offa's Dyke Path, John B. Jones, HMSO, 1976

The Pembrokeshire Coast Path, John H. Barrett, HMSO, 1974

Various booklets and leaflets published by The Department of the Environment, Local Councils and for other properties in private ownership.

Acknowledgements

I should like to express my sincere appreciation to the respective Deans of Cathedrals at Newport, Llandaff and St David's, for their permission to reproduce pictures of the interiors of these beautiful buildings. Also, to Cardiff City Council for 'installing' me in the lighting gantry at the Cardiff Searchlight Tattoo. Thanks are also due to the Management of Dan-yr-Ogof Showcaves, who provided facilities for the photography of the Cathedral Showcave, and to David Freeman, Keeper of Tredegar House, for allowing me to photograph The Gilt Room, and to crib from his excellent guide to Tredegar House.

I am also indebted to John Hodges and Michael Turner of Cwnfforest Riding Centre who, together with 'Princess', arranged the photograph on page 22.

Other backroom people who should be mentioned are Richard and Alison Neville, for providing speedy transport to South Wales on two occasions, Frank Nash for checking my typescript, and my mother who has corrected my suspect spelling.

The Publisher acknowledges the assistance of the Welsh Books Council in obtaining the Welsh translation of the introductory text and captions.

First published 1984

ISBN 0 86364 028 1

Photographs © Derek Forss 1984

© Town & County Books Ltd 1984

Published by Town & County Books Ltd, Shepperton, Surrey; and printed in Italy by Graphische Betriebe Athesia, Bolzano

Introduction

Although Snowdonia invariably claims the Bardic crown for Cymric scenic splendour South Wales is equally a region of extraordinary beauty and contrast. It also manages to absorb the greater part of the country's population in three large cities, and has, in the last century, seen dramatic changes in its environment, particularly in the mining valleys. This extraordinary contrast — coal mine and castle, mountain and industrial heartland — contributes enormously to its appeal; the very mountains seem to grow, quite naturally, out of the gardens of the industrial valleys.

For the purpose of this book South Wales includes the Brecon Beacons National Park. The author is well aware that some residents in the Brecon Beacons and Black Mountains prefer to associate themselves with mid-Wales and the northern part of their county — Brecknockshire. Although their views are valid and appreciated, the Usk — west of Brecon — and Wye river valleys do provide a natural demarcation line in purely geographical terms, where northward the land assumes a totally different character from anything else in South Wales.

South Wales has two National Parks to North Wales' one. These two Parks are utterly different. Pen-y-Fan is the highest point of the Brecon Beacons and South Wales. At 2,906ft it overlooks the neighbouring tops of Corn-du and Cribyn, and a walk over all three tops is a classic route for the hill-walking fraternity. In complete contrast, the Pembrokeshire Coast National Park has the most dramatic and continuous cliff scenery in Great Britain. A long distance footpath follows the indented shoreline and can be accomplished, in sections, by anyone familiar with country walking.

The first piece of 'Welsh-ness' encountered after crossing the Severn Bridge is Chepstow, but unfortunately, the motorway lures the traveller away from this border town. The old route used to pass through Gloucester, entering Wales by way of either Monmouth or Chepstow, the latter then being unavoidable for destinations in Newport and Cardiff. Between these two historic towns meanders the Wye, beloved of Wordsworth, threading its way to join the Severn and passing Wales' celebrated monastic house, Tintern Abbey.

Northwards and westwards from Chepstow, at the head of the Wye Valley, are the Black Mountains. Forming the eastern section of the Brecon Beacons National Park, these hills are really not as 'black' as the name might suggest; in fact they are very friendly hills. One theory for their austere name is explained by their prospect from the east, especially from the Malvern Hills, when against the setting sun, they do appear rather sombre. Although they are very much the preserve of walkers and pony trekkers, the Black Mountains also have a scenic drive through their eastern half. A narrow country lane leaves the A465 Abergavenny to Hereford road, through the Vale of Ewyas, to pass another well-known monastic house in Wales — Llanthony Priory — and finally traverses the truly spectacular Gospel Pass to the border town of Hay-on-Wye.

In this book, for the larger part of our imaginary journey from Chepstow, we have followed Offa's Dyke Long Distance Footpath. Offa, Saxon King of Mercia, built this great earthwork in the 8th century, to separate his kingdom, most of Central England, from Wales. The rampart and ditch of the dyke run almost continuously from the Severn to the Dee, and it was a happy inspiration for the footpath to follow its route. Although dedicated to the serious walker, certain lower stretches may be explored safely by surefooted family walkers.

Westward from the Black Mountains we enter the ancient Kingdom of Brycheinog, which, together with the other Kingdoms of Gwent, Morgannwg, and the southern parts of Seisyllwg and Deheubarth, forms an area roughly equivalent to present-day South Wales. It was Edward I who imposed the 'shires' on Wales, but it is still meaningful to speak of Pembrokeshire, Carmarthenshire, etc. The county reorganisation, and reversion to earlier regional names such as Dyfed, has met with some opposition; nevertheless, the 'old' county of Monmouthshire, now, 'returns' to Wales, reviving in the process, the name of Gwent. Brycheinog, and other parts of Brecknockshire, are swallowed up in the enormous county of Powys, which stretches beyond Welshpool. The 'shire' county names have been retained for the administrative regions within the county — hence, Radnor District in mid-Wales.

Brecon is the administrative town of the National Park, and appropriately, the mountains loom towards the town like the crest of a gigantic wave. The name Brecon, from which the mountain range takes its name, derives from Brycheinog, but the official Welsh name for the town has entirely different origins. Brecon lies at the meeting place of two rivers where the Honddu joins the Usk. The Welsh name from Brecon — *Aberhonddu*, refers to the confluence, or mouth (*aber*) of the river Honddu, which rises in Mynydd Eppynt to the north of the town. Other comparisons can be found in Swansea (*Abertawe*), and Fishguard (*Abergwaun*), but most English 'translations' are simply a corruption of the Welsh, hence Cardiff (*Caerdydd*) and Gower (*Gŵyr*).

Southwards, the Brecon Beacons dissolve into the mining valleys, the only visible division of any note being the 'Heads of the Valleys' road. A study of the Ordnance Survey map, published in the 1950s is fascinating. Then, almost every valley had its own railway line with many branch lines radiating from Cardiff and Newport, from where a new found wealth of shining black coal was exported. Now the passenger services are savagely cut to the Rhondda, Taff and Rhymney valleys, with the remaining lines dismantled or at best, operating only freight traffic.

Coal production in the South Wales mining valleys is now on the decline, bringing with it yet another dramatic change to the social climate. Industrialisation in the 19th century was just as devastating, but then it was the landscape which suffered where once stood trees in the green valleys of the Rhondda and Rhymney. The Wales Tourist Board are now just as anxious to direct the visitor to these valleys, where the collieries are closing one by one, to be replaced by other 'cleaner' industries. We are encouraged to sample superhighways, such as the new A470 out of Cardiff into the heart of the Taff Valley, past Castell Coch re-created in the 19th century. Further along, the roads, in the series of enormous hair-pin bends, climb mountain sides to 1,500ft or more. Below lie Treherbert and Treorchy, stretching in an unbroken line of terraced houses, the waste tips of coal mines, and the newer industrial estates; invariably separated from each other by rugby fields.

Another road out of Treorchy, again by a series of hair-pin bends, takes the motorist over Bwlch-y-Clawdd into Ogmore Vale and the Glamorgan coastline. The opening of this latest section of the M4 now relieves a picturesque area from traffic bound for Swansea, a city which has also witnessed many changes in recent years, particularly in the aftermath of the bombings in World War 2. Swansea offers many attractions. Near Dylan Thomas's birthplace rises one of the city's famous hills — Townhill with views over the whole of Swansea Bay. The city lies at our feet, and eastwards along the Glamorgan coast is Port Talbot with its steel works belching thick black smoke, contrasting with the green hills that almost shunt the town into the sea. Westwards, and again in contrast, the eye is led by the graceful curve of the bay to Mumbles and Gower. Gower could be referred to as Swansea's playground and how fortunate are both inhabitants of city and country. Gower packs a lot of good stuff into its compact form; here again is a peninsula offering variety with rugged seaward cliffs and opposite, sands on the Loughor Estuary.

Across the Loughor Estuary, and further round Carmarthen Bay to the estuaries of the Taf and Tywi, is Laugharne, a place of pilgrimage for all devotees of Dylan Thomas and his writings. His boat house and shed, where he wrote *Under Milkwood*, look out on a more pastoral scene where the mountains, that once were the Brecon Beacons and Black Mountain, have been tamed and subdued to the rolling green hills that surround Carmarthen.

The Pembrokeshire Coast National Park is the smallest National Park in Great Britain. Its protected area comprises the coast from Amroth to Cardigan, plus the Preseli Mountains in the northern part of the county. Milford Haven is one of our most impressive natural harbours, much of which is now given over to oil refineries. Further inland, but still within the Park, the Cleddau river and its many tributaries wind deeply into the county. For such a comparatively small area, Pembrokeshire possesses an amazing wealth of features. With a magnificent castle at Pembroke, and one of the most impressive neolithic burial chambers in the Preseli Mountains, not to mention St David's Cathedral and various islands dotted around the coast; it seems almost unfair that Pembrokeshire should also possess one of the finest seaside resorts in South Wales — Tenby. Slot machines and bingo are very low key in Tenby. Many people visit this ancient walled town in July and August and are offered the choice of two magnificent beaches, a picturesque harbour, and boat trips to Caldey Island. Tourists visiting Tenby for the first time will be confused by twisting narrow streets, winding in endless circular directions, until, quite bewildered, they become convinced that the town planners made a considerable mistake in the siting of St Mary's church and the congregation cannot possibly be facing east for prayer!

The highest point of Pembrokeshire is Foel-cwmcaerwyn, the summit of the Preseli Mountains, at 1,760ft. It is possible to avoid a climb by taking the Haverfordwest to Cardigan road which crosses these smooth, but steep hills at an altitude not much lower then this highest point. Mynydd Preseli has fascinated historians and geologists alike for many years, because Carnmenyn is believed to be the source of the massive bluestones that make up the inner circle of Stonehenge. The problem is how they got there. Although we may never find out for certain, the most popular theory is that they were transported from Milford Haven, by sea up the Bristol Channel, and with a superhuman effort, across land to Salisbury Plain.

In many respects, South Wales is just as cosmopolitan as any other area in Great Britain. The Welsh language is older in origin than English, and is a source of great national pride. At the moment the Welsh tongue is undergoing a revival hence its inclusion in this book, and in many local communities it can be heard in the shops and streets. A major stumbling block for English ears (and eyes), is the Welsh spelling with its proliferation of double 'lls' and 'dds' together with a heavy use of the letter 'y'. The fact that a 'c' is invariably pronounced as a 'k', and 'f' as a 'v', and a double 'ff' as an 'f', often throws the visitor into a state of confusion. Welsh is now taught (and used) in schools alongside English, and it would appear to be a decided advantage to learn the language at the earliest possible age. The Welsh are recognised internationally as a nation of singers, where the vernacular lends itself exceedingly well (and beautifully) to music.

After having travelled the industrial heartland in Glamorgan and Monmouthshire we arrive at St David's. The interior of the Cathedral has been likened to an Arabian palace and comes as a surprise after the comparative austerity of the exterior. In medieval times it must have been what Canterbury represented to travellers on the so-called Pilgrim's Way through Hampshire, Surrey and Kent. The 'cult' of St David spread throughout Wales in the mid-12th century and Pope Callixtus II decreed that two pilgrimages to St David's shrine equalled one to Rome. Some doubt remains that the precious casket in Holy Trinity Chapel still contains the bones of St David, although recent examination tends to support the theories of those historians who think it does.

For many visitors — and pilgrims, — to South Wales, St David's is the culmination, and perhaps finale, of their tour through the region. A short distance from the 'city', are the ruins of St Non's Chapel, the reputed birthplace of Wales' patron saint with all sorts of legends attached to this important event. The Department of the Environment, who maintain this sacred ruin, have unfortunately (though probably for very good reasons), erected one of their commercial standard fences around the site which does rather take away some of the grace and magic of the place. Nevertheless, with St David's, its cathedral and Bishops Palace, almost surrounded by Pembrokeshire's bewitching coastline, it has enough of Paradise about it to be long remembered with affection. Few people leave this little corner of Pembrokeshire (and even on a winter's day!), without a feeling of regret, and with hope that one day they will return. Here too we end our journey.

Derek Forss
Tŷddewi/Surrey Hills
1983

Rhagarweiniad

Ymestyn De Cymru o Gas-gwent yng Ngwent i Dyddewi yn Nyfed, ac o'r Gelli ym Mrycheiniog i'r Barri ym Morgannwg. I bwrpas y llyfr hwn mae De Cymru yn cynnwys Parc Cenedlaethol Bannau Brycheiniog, sydd yn gwbl wahanol i Barc Cenedlaethol Penfro. Pen-y-Fan yw'r mynydd uchaf yn y Bannau ac yn Ne Cymru, tra ym Mhenfro yr arfordir creigiog yw hynodrwydd y rhan honno o'r wlad.

Yng Ngwent fe geir cyfuniad o brydferthwch naturiol a hynafiaethau diddorol: cymoedd diwydiannol yn y gorllewin; arfordir Môr Hafren, a'r rhannau dwyreiniol, rhwng Wysg a Gwy, lle y mae tawelwch a llonyddwch gyda'r enwau lleoedd Cymraeg, er i'r heniaith gilio ers cenedlaethau bellach oddi ar wefusau'r trigolion.

Dyffryn Wysg yw craidd Brycheiniog yn Ne Powys, ac yma ceir peth o'r tir amaethyddol gorau yng Nghymru, gyda chribau'r Fforest Fawr a'r Bannau yn ymestyn am filltiroedd lawer ar yr ochr ddeheuol. Dyma fynydd-dir anial sydd hefyd yn cynnig cyfleusterau da i gerddwyr a merlotwyr.

I'r de gwelir y Bannau yn ymdoddi i'r dyffrynnoedd glofaol. Cymoedd cyfan wedi eu hanrheithio gan y Chwyldro Diwydiannol, ond yn sgîl y dirwasgiad yn y gweithfeydd glo bu cryn ddatblygu ar ddiwydiannau ysgafn yn ystod y degawdau diwethaf a chodwyd nifer o stadau diwydiannol yng nghysgod y pyllau a'r tipiau glo.

O'r cymoedd creithiog ewch i lawr i Fro Morgannwg â'i harfordir trawiadol. Yma mae prydferthwch a hynafiaethau'r Fro yn werth eu gweld, gyda phentrefi bychain o fythynnod to gwellt. Bydd ffresni ac unigedd Penrhyn Gŵyr hefyd yn falm i'r enaid blinedig.

Ar hyd yr arfordir i'r gorllewin fe geir gweld golygfa odidog o ddyffrynnoedd toreithiog Caerfyrddin yn ymdoddi i'r môr, a phentrefi pysgota deniadol fel Talacharn, cartref enwog Dylan Thomas.

Parc Cenedlaethol Penfro yw'r lleiaf ym Mhrydain, ond er hynny y mae'n cynnwys amrywiaeth fawr o olygfeydd: o fynyddoedd y Preseli yn y gogledd i glogwyni a chreigiau a thraethau godidog ar hyd ei lannau.

Wedi teithio o ganolfannau diwydiannol Gwent a Morgannwg sydd yn cynnwys tri chwarter poblogaeth Cymru, cyrhaeddwn Dyddewi. Pentref sydd hefyd yn ddinas am fod iddo eglwys gadeiriol. Yn sicr bydd cyrraedd y lle hwn yn uchafbwynt a diweddglo teilwng i'r daith drwy'r rhanbarth.

HEFIN LLWYD   7

Cas-gwent, Mynwy (Gwent) Adferwyd yr hen dref hon i Gymru drachefn.

Chepstow (Cas-gwent), Monmouthshire (Gwent) Until April 1974, Monmouthshire was politically part of England. After the re-organisation of county boundaries, Monmouthshire — now re-christened Gwent (an even earlier name) — was 'returned' to Wales — a change which still causes some problems for residents as to where their allegiance lies.

For motorists travelling to Wales, the obvious route from London is now over the Severn Bridge where the first town over the border is Chepstow, on the banks of the Wye. Previously, a ferry operated near the Bridge, otherwise the route lay via Gloucester to enter Wales over the Wye via an iron road bridge, one of the earliest in Britain and dating from 1816. For the majority who enter the Principality courtesy of the motorway, Chepstow is certainly well worth the diversion. There are several impressive features including a cliff-top castle and a town-gate, the latter still proving quite an obstacle to traffic in and out of Wales.

8

Abaty Tyndyrn, Mynwy (Gwent) Ar un cyfnod, hon oedd un o fynachlogydd pwysicaf ein gwlad.

Tintern Abbey (Tyndyrn), Monmouthshire (Gwent) Nestling in a wooded valley on the banks of the Wye, the ruins of Tintern Abbey come as a surprise to road users travelling from Chepstow to Monmouth. Tintern Abbey was founded in 1131 for monks of the Cistercian Order and rose to become one of the richest and most important monastic houses in Wales. Now in the care of The Department of the Environment, it attracts many visitors who come to appreciate the eye for beauty of the master masons who built it. An earlier visitor was William Wordsworth who pays tribute to Tintern and the River Wye with the following lines composed during his tour of 1793:

> *O sylvan Wye! thou wanderer thro'*
> *the woods,*
> *How often has my spirit turned to thee!*

Later, a railway was constructed through the valley but unhappily has now closed. No doubt Wordsworth would have rejoiced over its closure, but its hey-day is now regarded with envy by railway enthusiasts. Not far from Tintern Abbey, however, is a railway museum, with walks along the old track bed for those who wish to indulge in its former glories.

10

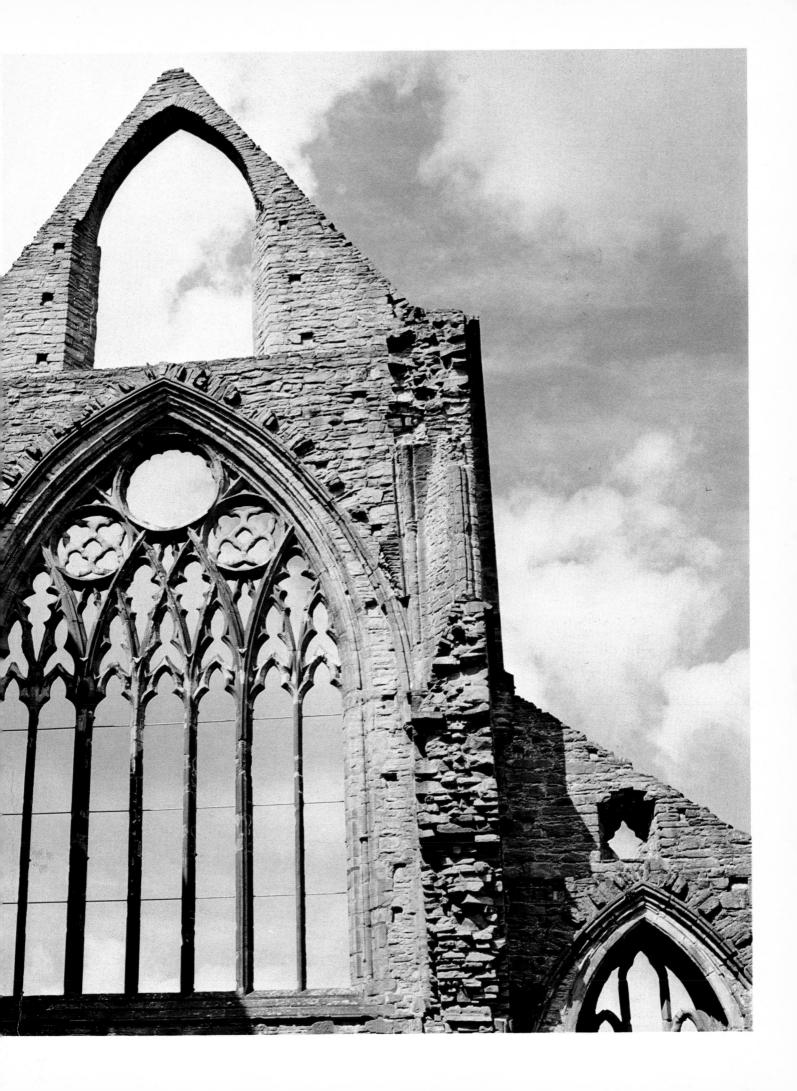

Trefynwy a Gatws Trefynwy (Gwent) Yr unig bont gaerog o'r oesoedd canol ym Mhrydain bellach.

Monmouth, Gwent 'The Monnow Bridge'
Another impressive border town near the Wye is Monmouth and just to the south of the town the Wye receives a tributary, the River Monnow, which rises in the Black Mountains. The Monnow Bridge, or gateway, is the only fortified bridge gateway in Great Britain and only one of a few in Europe. Built in 1262 it presents an imposing entrance to the town, now much relieved by the recent A40 by-pass. The main shopping street and countless narrow alley-ways are all worthy of a leisurely exploration.

The reddish-brown colouring of the water is caused by iron-oxide, and is the result of heavy over night rain, bringing sediment down from rocks of the Old Red Sandstone series. On occasions this dis-colouration even affects the household water supply in the area.

Llanddewi Nant Hodni, Mynwy (Gwent)
Priordy Normanaidd mewn llecyn tawel yn
Nyffryn Ewias.

Llanthony Priory (Llanddewi Nant Hodni),
Monmouthshire (Gwent)
  I loved thee by the streams of yore
  By distant streams I love thee more
Thus commented, with irony, the poet
Walter Savage Landor who, in 1807,
purchased the Abbey with the intention of
planning a model estate but it foundered on
bitter feuds with tenants and neighbours.

The Vale of Ewyas is a sylvan valley
running south to north on the eastern side
of the Black Mountains, but just inside the
boundary with Herefordshire. Offa's Dyke
Long Distance Footpath follows this
boundary and a minor road leaves the A465
Abergavenny to Hereford road, passing
through the vale to ascend the Gospel Pass.
Again, Llanthony Priory is popular with
tourists, and this lonely peaceful scene,
which ironically attracts many visitors, was
the inspiration early in the 12th century for
a religious settlement. Founded by a
Norman knight, William de Lacy, it was
eventually established as one of the very
few houses of the Augustinian order.

14

Bwlch yr Efengyl, Brycheiniog (Powys) O ben y bwlch ceir golygfa wych o diriondeb ffrwythlon Dyffryn Gwy a'r bryniau moelion y tu draw.

Gospel Pass, Brecknockshire, (Powys) The minor single track road through the Vale of Ewyas continues to follow the Afon Honddu (not to be confused with the Brecon Honddu), and climbs to 1,778ft at Gospel Pass. A number of parking places enables the motorist to share the exhilaration for mountain scenery normally reserved for hill-walkers, as the panorama dramatically unfolds northwards over Brecknockshire. On either hand are imposing mountains; Lord Hereford's Knob (2,263ft) and Hay Bluff (2,219ft), the latter a well known venue for hang gliders. Often in view are ponies belonging to the trekking centres which abound in this part of Wales.

Hay-on-Wye (Y Gelli), Brecknockshire (Powys). Hay-on-Wye has the unique distinction of claiming to be the second-hand book capital of Great Britain. Some inhabitants, through their publications, even claim independence from the rest of the country! It is yet another frontier town on the Wye, sheltered by the Black Mountains. Offa's Dyke Long Distance Footpath passes through it to continue its 168 mile journey, through the rolling Mid-Wales hills, to Pre-

statyn on the coast of North Wales. Those hardy walkers who decide to make Hay-on-Wye an overnight stop will find a multitude of bookshops on every corner, offering publications on every conceivable subject even to the abolition of the local tourist board!

There are other attractive features to catch the eye, not least the 'classic' town clock which dates from 1884.

Y Gelli, Brycheiniog (Powys). Yn enwog am ei siopau ail-law, ac am ei hannibyniaeth.

18

Y Grib, Y Mynydd Du, Brycheiniog (Powys)
Yr olygfa i gyfeiriad y gogledd dros ganolbarth Cymru o'r Waun Fach, y llecyn uchaf ar y Mynydd Du.

Y Grîb, The Black Mountains, Brecknockshire (Powys) The view, north-wards, over mid-Wales from Waun Fach, the highest point of the Black Mountains at 2,660ft. It is not the shapely mountain one would expect. Instead it is rather a featureless moor, which in winter is often unpleasantly boggy. Nevertheless, a traverse of this summit, taking in Pen Trumau and Y Grîb on the way, can be a rewarding and interesting excursion in the summer, particularly when Pen-y-Fan is resembling Porthcawl in sheer numbers.

Y Grîb is undoubtedly the highlight of this walk where a ridge offering a switchback ride leads to Castell Dinas and the main road. Northwards, there is an uninterrupted view over mid-Wales and the Wye Valley with the river threading its way past Hay-on-Wye after passing Builth Wells, further to the north. Westwards, the view includes the Brecon Beacons, Pen-y-Fan being the main feature. Mynydd Troed, which looks a magnificent mountain from the approaches at Talgarth, looks quite insignificant from the superior Y Grîb.

Cwmfforest, Brycheiniog (Powys) Ardal sy'n cynnig cyfleusterau da i ferlotwyr.

Cwmfforest, Brecknockshire (Powys) A car journey along the Crickhowell to Talgarth road will reveal several pony trekking establishments displaying their signboards and, in some parts, bridleways dedicated to, and specially provided for, the convenience of horse riders. At Cwmfforest, near Pengenfford, preparations are well under-way for the new season. 'Princess' patiently waits whilst her master prepares for the all-important grooming session.

22

Castell Dinas, Brycheiniog (Powys) Anialdir uchel ac anghyfannedd Y Mynydd Du, ond sydd er hynny yn atyniad i gerddwyr.

Castell Dinas, Brecknockshire (Powys)
Residents of the higher regions of the Black Mountains often surprise their visitors by stating that spring in this area comes at least one month late. While the trees by the River Usk are here in spring leaf, the trees on the slopes of Mynydd Troed or Castell Dinas hardly show any sign of budding. The Black Mountains range, together with the whole of the Brecon Beacons National Park, is a mecca for walkers, but on ground above 1,500ft Arctic conditions often previal during winter months. Mountain accidents are not uncommon within the Park and this picture of Castell Dinas, an ancient hill fort, brings the whole matter sharply into perspective. Modest in altitude, it was photographed on 21 April, a full month after the official first day of spring.

24

Llyn Syfaddan, Brycheiniog (Powys) Llyn naturiol mwyaf De Cymru a orwedd mewn cylch o fryniau cysgodol, ac sy'n enwog am ei chwedlau.

Llangorse Lake (Llyn Syfaddan), Brecknockshire (Powys) The largest natural lake in South Wales, Llangorse has its own fair share of legends; from sunken palaces to eerie voices and blood flowing in the lake. Although the first of these legends has never been substantiated to any degree, there are certainly valid reasons for the other strange occurrences. It has been suggested that the cracking and heaving of winter ice could have given rise to those weird human like noises, whilst the River Llyfni, entering Llangorse Lake from the South, bringing with it iron-oxide deposits, has caused the 'blood' colouration of the water.

In view, snow topped Mynydd Troed (1,997ft) acts as sentinel to this peaceful scene on an early spring morning, before the waters are disturbed by sailors and canoeists. Also nearby, and on the south side of the lake is the picturesque church of Llangesty, built around 1848.

Crucywel, Brycheiniog (Powys) Un o dreflannau'r Gororau; gwelir yma bont hyfryd ac iddi dri bwa ar ddeg.

Crickhowell (Crucywel), Brecknockshire (Powys) Crickhowell is one of those places you seem to pass through on your way to greater things, without bothering to stop. It is, however, pleasantly situated on the River Usk, in the shadow of Table Mountain — a hill of slightly lower elevation than its more famous brother in distant Cape Town.

At one time the town was noted for the manufacture of Crickhowell flannel, but this industry largely died out in the 1830s. Today, Crickhowell presents its pictorial front well away from the main road, down by the Usk where a 13 arch bridge (or is it twelve), spans the water with town and church forming the middle background.

Pen-y-Fâl, Y Fenni, Mynwy (Gwent) Gall cerddwyr llai profiadol fentro i gopa'r mynydd ar dywydd teg i werthfawrogi'r golygfeydd dros Y Fenni a thu draw i Sir Gaerloyw.

The Sugar Loaf, Abergavenny (Y Fenni), Monmouthshire (Gwent) The Black Mountains are essentially the preserve of hardier walkers and pony trekkers from the riding centres and paths and bridleways criss-cross the hills. For the less hardy individual a taste for the hills can be experienced by taking a very steep and narrow road out of Abergavenny, signposted 'Sugar Loaf'. This road does not take you right on to the Sugar Loaf, but to a car park on Llanwenarth Common where the walk to the summit begins — most of the climbing having been accomplished in the car.

The Sugar Loaf (1,995ft) should not be attempted if the weather is inclement, but most people will be satisfied with this view from the Common, showing the ground gently rising to the distinctive summit. In the opposite direction, and a few steps to the east, are extensive views over Abergavenny and, on exceptionally clear days, beyond into Gloucestershire.

30

Eglwys Gadeiriol Gwynllyw, Casnewydd-ar-Wysg, Mynwy (Gwent) Saif ar fryn uwchlaw'r dref; y mae yn ei phensaernïaeth gyfuniad o'r hen a'r newydd.

St Woolos Cathedral Newport (Casnewydd-ar-Wysg), Monmouthshire (Gwent)
Ancient and modern, modest in proportions, the cathedral church of St Woolos stands on a ridge overlooking the busy town of Newport. St Woolos was raised to full cathedral status in 1949 and during 1960-1962 the chancel, which the Victorians had previously restored, was entirely rebuilt. Designed by John Piper, with the mural executed by the scenery painters of the Royal Opera House, Covent Garden, this new chancel now provides a striking contrast when viewed from the Gallilee Chapel, through the Norman arch and down the nave. Unlike many other modern additions, this improvement blends well with the present building — itself featuring many styles over the centuries — and holds the attention of all pilgrims who enter by the west door.

Yr Ystafell Euraid, Plas Tredegar, Casnewydd-ar-Wysg, Mynwy (Gwent) Ystafell ysblennydd hen gartref Arglwydd Tredegar; ar agor i'r cyhoedd, a than ofal Cyngor Bwrdeistref Casnewydd.

The Gilt Room, Tredegar House Newport (Casnewydd-ar-Wysg), Monmouthshire (Gwent) Much of Newport owes its existence to the Morgan family, later Lords of Tredegar. Their wealth included properties in the shires of Brecknock, Glamorgan and Monmouth, much of it yielding iron and coal. Newport therefore, became a distribution centre requiring the development of canals, roads and railways as means of transportation. Tredegar House, just to the west of the town, and quite near the new motorway, was the family's magnificent country house. It was designed to impress, but between 1951, when the last of the Morgan family left the property, until 1974, it served as a school. Today, Tredegar House is undergoing extensive restoration and refurbishing and is in the care of Newport Borough Council. It is open to the public who can also stroll in the adjoining grounds and gardens.

The Gilt Room probably served as a reception room to which the assembled company retired after dinner on formal occasions.

Castell Caerffili, Caerffili, Morgannwg Tref enwog am ei chaws a'i chastell, yr adfail milwrol ail fwyaf ym Mhrydain.

Caerphilly Castle, Caerphilly (Caerffili), Glamorgan The name Caerphilly inevitably comes to mind in connection with a white, crumbly cheese (rarely made in this area now), and to an enormous and impressive castle, the second largest in Great Britain. Dominating the township, Caerphilly Castle is one of those monuments that 'Cromwell knocked about a bit'. It features a leaning tower standing as testimony to the superior design of the castle, or the inferiority of Cromwellian gunpowder. Originally, this fortification was one of many castles built to encircle and garrison Wales. Other examples of notable edifices of this period in South Wales include those at Kidwelly, Cardigan, Newport, Grosmont, St Quintin's, Ogmore and Cardiff.

Tatŵ Chwilolau Caerdydd, Morgannwg
Arddangosfa odidog a gynhelir yng Nghastell
Caerdydd am wythnos bob Awst.

*Cardiff Searchlight Tattoo Cardiff
(Caerdydd), Glamorgan* Described by the
promoters as 'Britain's Greatest', the Cardiff
Searchlight Tattoo is a spectacular display
of military precision and stirring music
performed by massed bands numbering
several hundred musicians. There are also
thrilling displays by the individual armed
services, often involving dogs, horses and
motor-bikes.

The focal point for this occasion, which
takes place for one week in August every
other year, is Cardiff Castle near the city's
shopping centre. All performers combine for
the Finale Muster Parade, where the enormous arena is entirely filled with uniformed
servicemen, providing a colourful and
rousing conclusion to the show. Audience
and performers all join forces to sing *Cwm
Rhondda* and *Hen Wlad fy Nhadau* (Land of
my Fathers).

38

Eglwys Gadeiriol Llandaf, Morgannwg Er ei difrodi gan fomiau rhyfel fe'i hadferwyd a cheir ynddi gerflun mawreddog Epstein, y 'Majestas'.

Llandaff Cathedral, Glamorgan Situated just to the north west of Cardiff city centre, stands the cathedral at Llandaff. This quiet, tranquil setting was shattered in January 1941 by enemy bombs which severely damaged the roof. Only Coventry Cathedral suffered heavier war damage, but the restoration at Llandaff now features among its new treasures, Epstein's *Christ in Majesty*.

Upon entering the west door the eye is immediately lifted upwards to this 'statue', for in reality it conceals the organ pipes. Epstein's creation divides its critics — for as many people who admire this work, you will find the same number who hate it.

*Plas y Dyffryn, Sain Nicolas, ger Caerdydd,
Morgannwg* Fe'i defnyddir fel canolfan
gynadleddau a chyrsiau, ac un o'i nodweddion arbennig yw ei erddi.

*Dyffryn House St Nicholas, near Cardiff,
Glamorgan* Dyffryn House is one of several
examples of a 'stately home' now used for a
different purpose. It was built in 1883 for
John Cory, whose heir, Reginald Cory, was
responsible for the magnificent gardens.
Now owned by Cardiff City Council, Dyffryn
House is used as a conference centre. The
gardens are still beautifully maintained by
the Council and are open during the
summer months.
   Dyffryn House is reached from the A48, a
few miles west of Cardiff, turning left on to
a minor road at St Nicholas.

Castell Ogwr, Morgannwg Adfeilion y castell mewn llecyn dymunol ar fin yr afon.

Ogmore Castle (Ogwr), Glamorgan To the south-west of Bridgend, lies the tiny community of Ogmore, near the point where the river, of the same name, reaches the Bristol Channel. Although not extensive, Ogmore Castle is the focal point of the area and together with the river, provides a scene of considerable charm. The remaining structure dates from the 12th century. Originally this fortress was one of three defending the fertile lands of The Vale of Glamorgan (the other two being at Coity and Newcastle [Bridgend]).

Just around the corner is Ogmore-by-Sea, a quiet, relatively unspoilt seaside village, and further inland is the unusual structure of Ewenny Priory.

44

Merthyr Mawr, Morgannwg Un o bentrefi prydferthaf Bro Morgannwg, gyda'i fythynnod to gwellt, a'i dwyni tywod uchel.

Merthyr Mawr, Glamorgan Across the stepping stones near Ogmore Castle, a delightful path leads to Merthyr Mawr. Featured in this village are several cottages with thatched roofs, an uncommon sight in Wales. Merthyr Mawr certainly has claims as one of the prettiest spots in Glamorgan and just to the south of the village, beyond the church, the farmlands quickly give way to extensive sand-dunes effectively separating Merthyr Mawr from the more 'modern' attractions at Porthcawl.

Merthyr Mawr is timeless and deserves a quiet inspection. Of particular interest are the sand dunes of Merthyr Mawr Warren which are among the highest in the country and popular for the unusual sport of sand tobogganing. These same sand hills are subject to erosion and movement by the south westerly gales sweeping in from the Atlantic and have yielded many fascinating archeological remains.

46

Bwlch y Clawdd, Morgannwg Ceir golygfa eang o ben y bwlch i gyfeiriad Cwm Rhondda a Threorci — ardaloedd y pyllau glo.

Bwlch-y-Clawdd, Glamorgan The road systems in South Wales are in many respects quite spectacular, and none more so than in the mining valleys. The main road leaving Ogmore Vale ascends the steep sided hills by an impressive series of hairpin bends to about 1,500ft only then to zig-zag down in similar spectacular fashion to the Rhondda Valley at Treorchy. At the summit of the pass, Bwlch-y-Clawdd, there is a lay-by from which are extensive views northwards to the Rhondda Valley with the terraced houses of Treorchy far below. These roads, together with the marvellous views, stand as testimony to the skills of yesterday's road engineers, and the local council has provided suitable inscriptions drawing the travellers' attention to the wonders of nature, now more widely appreciated through man's ingenuity.

48

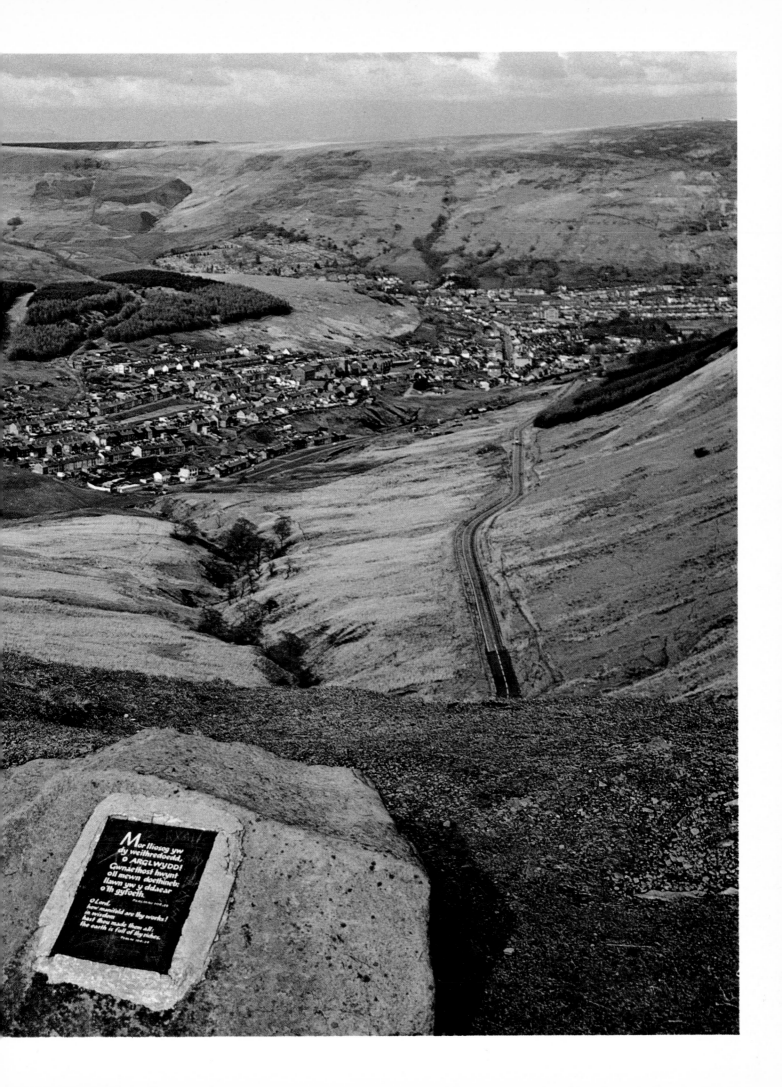

Mor lliosog yw
dy weithredoedd,
O ARGLWYDD!
Gwnaethost hwynt
oll mewn doethineb:
llawn yw y ddaear
o'th gyfoeth.
Psalm 104:24

O Lord,
how manifold are thy works!
in wisdom
hast thou made them all:
the earth is full of thy riches.
Psalm 104:24

Rhondda Fach, Morgannwg Cysylltir y Rhondda a'r cymoedd cyfagos â'r diwydiant glo, ac ynddynt ceir cymdeithas glòs iawn.

Little Rhondda Valley (Rhondda Fach), Glamorgan The Rhondda Valley, perhaps above all others, is associated with the times when coal was king. In reality however, because the coal measures lie a good distance below the surface of this valley, development came late. Nevertheless, from a population of around 1,000 in 1851, it rose to its peak of 163,000 in 1951. Today, in the Rhondda, men still toil for the fuel of our present industry, but the boom is well past. Many of the collieries have closed with much of the land allocated for alternative use.

These valleys possess a community which is close knit politically and culturally, and even in times of recession the people can offer the visitor a cheerful welcome. An inseparable institution much associated with this area is the Welsh male voice choir, Treorchy being a household name. Although basically an amateur choir, they have recorded for Columbia and His Master's Voice records, and tour the country extensively.

50

Comin Hirwaun, Morgannwg Mae ffyrdd troellog yn nodweddiadol o'r cymoedd glo; arweiniant at flaenau'r dyffrynnoedd, a Bannau Brycheiniog yn gefndir hardd.

Hirwaun Common, Glamorgan At Treherbert, the road northwards from the Rhondda Valley, ascends by a route once more typical of the South Wales mining area. After a succession of tortuous hair-pin bends, and a long haul to the summit of the pass, Llyn Fawr Reservoir comes into view, and further northwards, Hirwaun Common stretches to the bleak town of Hirwaun with the Brecon Beacons forming a classic backdrop. Again, parking places are provided by the roadside for the fullest appreciation of this remarkable view, with the main road executing a double loop beneath our feet as it proceeds to the 'Heads of the Valleys' road.

52

Bannau Brycheiniog o Fynydd Illtud, Brycheiniog (Powys) Mynyddoedd i'w cerdded yw'r Bannau, gan fod craig y tywodfaen coch yn rhy fregus i ddringwyr.

The Brecon Beacons from Mynydd Illtyd, Brecknockshire (Powys) For travellers on the A470 road from Builth Wells, the Brecon Beacons seem appear to make a sudden and dramatic appearance but more often than not, these distinctive mountains are enshrouded in mist, and even in the height of summer, visibility can be considerably impaired by heat-haze.

Pen-y-Fan is the highest point in South Wales at 2,906ft and together with its near neighbours — Cribyn to the east and Corn-du to the west — provide the experienced walker with a most rewarding day on the hills.

The views on a fine day from the summit are extensive, and on exceptionally clear days, Cader Idris in the Snowdonia National Park can be discerned just to the right of Plynlimon. During the Ice Age, glaciers gouged these northern slopes into great basins or cwms leaving lakes such as Llyn-cwm-llwch. The present viewpoint at Mynydd Illtyd is, however, within the reach of most mortals where a moorland road from Brecon provides unrestricted views towards the Beacons.

Pen-y-Fan o lethrau'r Cribyn, Bannau Brycheiniog. Dyma'r mynydd uchaf yn y De, gyda'r golygfeydd godidog o'i gopa.

Pen-y-Fan from the slopes of Cribyn, Brecon Beacons, Brecknockshire, (Powys) The awesome face of Pen-y-Fan, now in shadow, frowns on a lone walker, minute in comparison.

Pen-y-Fan at 2,906ft is the highest mountain in Britain south of Cader Idris near Dolgellau. In clear weather the view from its summit includes the Cader Idris range to the North West, across the Bristol Channel to the hills of Somerset and Devon, and the Malvern Hills.

56

*Ogof yr Eglwys Gadeiriol, Dan-yr-Ogof,
Glyntawe, Brycheiniog* Yr ogofau
tanddaearol mwyaf ym Mhrydain, a gellir eu
gweld yng ngolau llif-oleuadau cryfion.

*The Cathedral Cave, Dan-yr-Ogof Caves,
Glyntawe, Brecknockshire (Powys)* At
Glyntawe are the spectacular underground
caves of Dan-yr-Ogof, reputed to be the
largest caverns in Great Britain. What is on
public show is a tiny part of the immense
labyrinth of interlinking caves. The
Cathedral Showcave, illuminated by power-
ful floodlights, have named features — 'The
Dome of St Paul's', the 'Cathedral Organ
pipes, and Nature's Painting are examples.

   Dan-yr-Ogof was not explored until the
1930s and further discoveries are still
taking place. It is doubtful however whether
the more remote caverns will ever be
opened to the public because of the
difficulty of access. Some guided tours are
available in other sections of the less
difficult caves.

Afon Mellte, Ystradfellte, Brycheiniog Ardal adnabyddus am ei rhyfeddodau naturiol, ei rhaeadrau a'i hogofeydd a'i hafonydd diflanedig.

Afon Mellte, Ystradfellte, Brecknockshire (Powys) High above the Vale of Neath, the infant streams feeding the river Neath have their humble beginnings in that vast tract of land, Fforest Fawr. The Afton Mellte is just one of these enchanting streams which near Ystradfellte, enters limestone country where there is a series of underground channels and waterfalls. Here is some of the least known yet most charming waterfall scenery in the country. From the car-park at Porth-yr-Ogof, the walker can explore this riverside scenery as the turbulent waters of the Mellte hurry to join their sister river.

A word of warning, however. This beautiful setting is not as innocuous as may first seem. It owes its beauty to the limestone formations which, although fascinating to the eye, can make walking somewhat hazardous. There is a proper path, but at times the sharp changes of level of the terrain make the wearing of stout shoes — or better, boots — highly essential.

Rhaeadr Clyn-gwyn, Brycheiniog Un o gyfres o raeadrau (neu 'sgydau' i arfer y gair lleol).

Clyn-gwyn Falls, Brecknockshire, (Powys)
A mile or so from the previous picture, the Afon Mellte takes on an entirely different character. In a narrow wooded gorge the river enters a succession of three waterfalls, of which the second is depicted.

One of the most favourable times to view these cascades is after a night of heavy rain and, perhaps, in spring when the foliage does not obstruct the view. However, on any fine day this is an attractive scene which repays the effort. From here, the Afon Mellte joins the River Neath and continues in a more industrial landscape before reaching the Bristol Channel.

Y Mynydd Du o Garreg Cennen, Caerfyrddin (Dyfed) Mynydd Du, Sir Gaerfyrddin, yw terfyn gorllewinol Parc Cenedlaethol Bannau Brycheiniog.

The Black Mountain from Carreg Cennen, Carmarthenshire (Dyfed) The Carmarthen Black Mountain — not to be confused with the Black Mountains in Brecknock and Monmouthshire — forms the western boundary of the Brecon Beacons National Park. The Park conveniently covers the area north of the 'Heads of the Valleys' road, the A465 Neath to Abergavenny. Geologically the area consists of rock from the Old Red Sandstone Series (Devonian), presenting a pronounced escarpment which faces north and gives the area its distinctive profile.

Running through the National Park is a small area of limestone rock, causing dramatic waterfalls and caverns as exhibited at Ystradfellte and Dan-yr-Ogof. West of the Black Mountain lofty summits give way to gentler and pastoral land as it reaches the river valleys cut by the Tywi and Loughor.

Castell Carreg Cennen, Llandeilo, Caerfyrddin Adfail castell Cymreig yn codi'n urddasol uwchben clogwyni uchel o galch-faen.

Carreg Cennen Castle, Llandeilo Carmarthenshire (Dyfed) Carreg Cennen Castle atop its towering crag must surely be one of the most dramatically situated fortresses in Britain. It is entirely isolated. To get there a car is essential (the nearest bus route is miles away) and even then a stiff climb has to be tackled from the car-park. However, the views toward the Black Mountain and into West Wales are superb.

The first fortress was originally built by the Welsh, but the present building dates from around 1283. The castle is of great interest to students of castle defence and has many unusual features including a 'secret passage'. Because of its isolated position, running water must have been a problem and it is assumed that rainwater must have been used. However, even with Wales' high rainfall, it is difficult to see how this alone could have sufficed to meet the needs of the garrison. The castle was demolished in 1462 after the Wars of the Roses to prevent its use as a hiding place for robbers.

Y Mwmbwls, Morgannwg Lle glan-môr atyniadol gyda chastell ac eglwys hynafol, ac angorfa i longau hwylio.

The Mumbles, Glamorgan The Mumbles are situated at the point where Swansea ends and Gower begins. The name, 'The Mumbles' is something of a mystery and refers specifically to the two rocky islands, one housing a lighthouse. A railway once ran from Swansea, along the entire length of the bay to the Mumbles pier. It was closed in 1960.

The Mumbles, together with Oystermouth, presents the fashionable aspect of Swansea. There are pleasant and well-kept gardens, an imposing castle at Oystermouth, and a yachting centre. Behind the main road that encircles Swansea Bay is a fascinating retreat of quiet alleyways and narrow streets. The Mumbles caters for many tastes, including those who simply wish to get away from it all. That wish is easily satisfied by rounding Mumbles Head where the coastal footpath begins and follows Gower's rocky coastline to Worms Head.

68

Carreg Arthur, Cefn Bryn, Gŵyr, Morgannwg Gellir gweld Penrhyn Gŵyr i gyd ar ddiwrnod clir, ac mae'r ardal gyfagos yn gyforiog o feini o gyfnod cynnar Cristnogaeth.

Arthur's Stone Cefn Bryn, Gower (Gŵyr), Glamorgan Inland, rising above Reynold-ston, is the long ridge of Cefn Bryn, quite modest in height, but with extensive views. A minor road crosses Cefn Bryn, so these views can be enjoyed by everyone, and the entire Gower Peninsula can be studied on a clear day.

From the car-park a path leads north-wards to Arthur's Stone, a prominent landmark enshrouded in mystery and legend. The capstone of millstone grit, was split, according to legend, by Arthur's sword Excalibur. The stone is said also to go down to the sea to drink on New Year's Eve.

Eglwys Porth-Einion, Gŵyr, Morgannwg
Pentref bychan glan-môr ar ddiwedd y brif-
ffordd sy'n rhedeg drwy Benrhyn Gŵyr.

*Port-Eynon Church, Gower (Gŵyr),
Glamorgan* Port-Eynon is a small seaside
village at the end of the main road through
Gower — a road which at times is hardly
wide enough to allow two cars to pass. The
centre-piece of the village is the church
with a life-size memorial outside it to a
lifeboat hero, Billy Gibbs, who was
coxswain of the Port-Eynon lifeboat when it
met disaster attempting a rescue in 1916.

From Port-Eynon Point, the headland to
the west of the village, lies Gower's
dramatic and celebrated coastline. One
local curiosity is Culver Hole, a deep cleft in
the rocks sealed off by rough masonry into
which the sea rushes at high water. It may
have been built by a local swashbuckler,
John Lucas, in the 16th century.

TO
THE GLORY OF GOD
AND IN MEMORY OF
WILLIAM (BILLY) GIBBS, COXSWAIN.
WILLIAM EYNON, SECOND COXSWAIN.
GEORGE HARRY, LIFEBOATMAN.
WHO WERE DROWNED OFF PWLL-DU
ON 1ST JANUARY 1916 WHEN THE PORTEYNON
LIFEBOAT "JANET" TWICE CAPSIZED IN THE
ENDEAVOUR TO RENDER ASSISTANCE
TO THE S.S. "DUNVEGAN."

THE SURVIVING MEMBERS OF THE CREW
CAPTN GEO. EYNON, WM. GROVE SEN.
WM. GROVE, JUN. ONSLOW GROVE,
WM. HARRIS, WM. POVEY
JOHN JENKINS, JAS. JENKINS,
LEONARD JENKINS, JOHN MORRIS,
AFTER GREAT SUFFERING SUCCEEDED IN
LANDING AT MUMBLES THE FOLLOWING MORNING.
THE BODIES OF WM. EYNON AND GEO. HARRY
WERE EVENTUALLY RECOVERED AND ARE
INTERRED IN THIS CHURCHYARD.

*Gŵyr; arfordir Morganwwg rhwng trwyn
Porth-Einon a Phen Pyrod* Ceir arfordir heb
ei well oddi yma i Ben Pyrod, a llwybr diogel
i'w gerdded. Islaw ceir Ogofau Paviland, lle
darganfyddwyd gweddillion dyn cyn-hanes,
a'r rheini wedi eu staenio'n goch.

*Gower (Gŵyr), Glamorganshire Coastline
between Port-Eynon Point and Worms
Head* Gower's thrilling coastline offers a
comparison to Pembrokeshire's equally
spectacular scenery. This viewpoint is about
one mile west of Port-Eynon, from the
footpath from Mumbles to Worms Head.
The vantage point cannot be reached by
car, but the path is relatively easy. In view
are limestone cliffs with their fascinating
tilted strata adding interest to the scene.

   Near this spot are Paviland Caves where,
in 1823, a headless skeleton was dis-
covered. It was originally called the 'Red
Lady of Paviland' because the bones had
been dyed with red ochre. Later it was
found to be the skeleton of a young man
ritually buried at a time when mammoths
and woolly rhinoceroses still roamed the
74 earth.

Bae Mewslade, Gŵyr, Morgannwg Ar droed yn unig y gellir mynd ato, a chredir mai hwn yw'r bae gorau ar Benrhyn Gŵyr.

Mewslade Bay, Gower (Gŵyr), Glamorgan
Mewslade Bay, the last southward facing bay before Worms Head, is attainable only on foot and is said to be the most spectacular in Gower. To the east, is Thurbla Head, 200ft high which is now owned by the National Trust. Built of limestone, it has an Iron Age fort as its crest.

76

Bae Rhosili, Gŵyr, Morgannwg Un o draethau tywod gorau Cymru; gellir gweld gweddillion llongau a ddrylliwyd ar y lan pan fydd y môr ar drai.

Rhossili Bay, Gower (Gŵyr), Glamorgan
The road from Port-Eynon to Rhossili ends abruptly on the cliff-top overlooking Rhossili Bay. Below is one of Wales' finest sandy beaches, facing westwards, protected by Worms Head and Burry Holms (the latter a bird sanctuary), on either side. Rhossili Down, Gower's highest point at 632ft (193m), shelters Rhossili Bay from the east.

In Rhossili Bay distances are deceptive. So open and immense is the seascape, that a walk from south to north across the bay, will invariably take twice the amount of time envisaged. Stronger walkers who can complete the circuit may like to consider a return traverse over bracing Rhossili Down, where the path leads unerringly back to the village.

Half buried in the sand at the bay's southern end and visible at low tide are the remains of an early shipwreck, the *Helvetia* wrecked in 1887. There have been many wrecks on this shore, however, and the most famous was the ship bringing back the dowry of Catherine of Braganza, Charles IIs queen. Silver dollars were washed ashore in the 19th century which provoked a local silver rush.

Y 'Boat House', Talacharn, Caerfyrddin (Dyfed) Dyma gartref Dylan Thomas, awdur *Under Milk Wood*, ac sydd bellach yn amgueddfa er cof amdano.

The Boat House, Laugharne (Lacharn), Carmarthenshire (Dyfed)

And some, like myself, just came, one day, for the day, and never left; got off the bus, and forgot to get on again.

Laugharne has become a pilgrimage for all admirers of Dylan Thomas, for here the visitor will find his boat house and shed where he wrote *Under Milkwood*. This idyllic spot saw the creation of such characters as Organ Morgan, Nogood Boyo & Mrs Ogmore-Pritchard, and both shed and boat house are open as a museum honouring his name. (He is buried in the local churchyard under a plain wooden cross.)

Laugharne's location — on the banks of the Taf — is, in some aspects, quite different from the rest of South Wales so far featured in this book, and that of Pembrokeshire to follow. A much greener and sylvan countryside is encountered and the hills, if they exist, are much less rugged. The boat house is approached from Laugharne village by a very narrow lane — with no turning places.

My seashaken house on a breakneck of rocks...

80

Bae Saundersfoot, Penfro (Dyfed) Cyrchfan
gwyliau pologaidd lle ceir traeth ysblennydd.

Saundersfoot Bay, Pembrokeshire (Dyfed)
The wide sweep of Carmarthen Bay contains many other fine smaller bays, coves
and river estuaries. One such bay is found at
Saundersfoot with excellent facilities for
visitors — all the more surprising since this
area was once a coal town in the 19th
century providing a high quality anthracite.

A popular footpath links Saundersfoot
with Tenby via Monkstone Point and passes
through coastal scenery which, although
lacking the full dramatic quality seen further
westwards, is charming in its own right. On
a clear day Gower is on the horizon to the
east and, after circumnavigation of the
headland, Caldey Island glints in the sun
beyond Tenby. On more dramatic days rain-
bows are a common sight in the bay.

82

Dinbych-y-Pysgo, Penfro (Dyfrd)   Tref glan-môr ddelfrydol, gyda'i harbwr, ei chastell ar gopa'r bryn, a'r hen furiau o'r bymthegfed ganrif yn ei hamgylchynu.

Tenby (Dinbych-y-pysgood),
Pembrokeshire (Dyfed)
   The most agreeable town on all the sea coast of South Wales, except Pembroke.
                                    Daniel Defoe
Tenby is an ancient walled town jealously guarded by local conservationists from the more modern forms of architectural invasion. Overlooked by numerous elegant Georgian houses — most of them are hotels nowadays — the charming harbour is an artist's delight. Tenby is an ancient settlement — probably established by the Vikings. The Normans seized and built a castle on the headland parts of which still stand. It became a walled town in the Middle Ages and changed hands several times in the Civil War to the detriment of its castle and its walls. When seaside watering places became popular in the Regency period, a local magnate saw its potential and provided it with its present elegant waterfront.

Codiad haul ar *Draeth y De, Dinbych-y-Pysgod.*

Sunrise on South Beach Tenby (Dinbych-y-pysgood), Pembrokeshire (Dyfed)
  My Lord what a Mornin'
The Welsh male choirs seem to be at their best, not only in the traditional Welsh hymn, but also in the Negro spiritual. The Tenby Male Choir are no exception; perhaps they are inspired by scenes like this sunrise on the expansive south beach.

86

Ynys Bŷr, Penfro (Dyfed) Mae'r ynys ramantus hon tua dwy filltir i'r de o Ddinbych-y-Pysgod, ond gellir ei chyrraedd gyda chwch.

Caldey Island (Ynys Pŷr), Pembrokeshire (Dyfed) Lying about two miles south of Tenby and separated from the mainland by a narrow tide-swept sound, Caldey Island has an other-worldly atmosphere about it that since time immemorial has attracted religious communities. The Benedictines established a monastery on the island in 1113 and remained until the Dissolution in 1534. Their buildings — refectory, gatehouse and prior's lodging — have survived. The Benedictines returned to Caldey early this century and they built the present Priory. When they moved to Prinknash in Gloucestershire in 1929, the Cistercians — a strict order also known as Trappists — took over and the island remains their property.

Caldey can be visited by boat from Tenby.

88

The Priory, Caldey Island (Ynys Pŷr), Pembrokeshire (Dyfed) The present religious community on Caldey was established in 1929. Dark-robed monks of the Cistercian Order successfully farm the land, manufacture their own brand of perfume, sold on the island, as well as in Tenby. Life on Caldey is in some aspects quite severe. Rising time, at all times of the year, is 3.15am; and the monks' diet is austere. Only men are permitted to visit the inside of the monastery buildings. The tour includes the refectory, sparsely laid out for evening meal, but with a surprise addition of modern sound equipment for the playing of gramophone records on Sunday afternoons.

Much of the day is taken by periods of devotion and these are held within the chapel which reflects the simplicity and frugality of the Trappist way of life. In contrast, the welcome extended to visitors is both genuine and warm.

Priordy, Ynys Bŷr, Penfro (Dyfed) Mae'r mynaich Sistersaidd yn gwbl hunan-gynhaliol, ac yn enwog am gynhyrchu persawr; dim ond dynion gaiff fynediad i weld yr abaty.

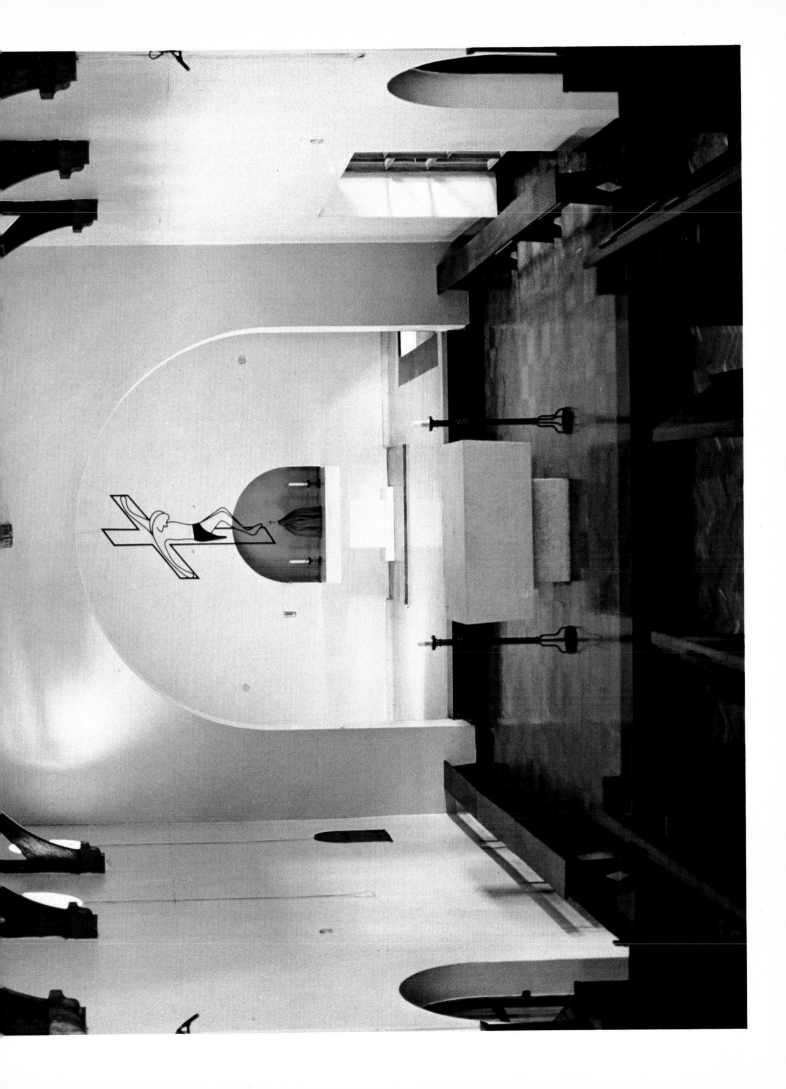

Trwyn Lydstep, Penfro (Dyfed) Mae'r pentir hwn yn eiddo i'r Ymddiriedolaeth Genedlaethol, a gellir cael mynediad i'r ogofau pan fydd y llanw ar drai.

Lydstep Point, Pembrokeshire (Dyfed)
Lydstep Point is a magnificent rocky head-land, with fine views towards Caldey Island (on the left) and the mysterious St Margaret's Island (on the right) and impres-sive limestone scenery. Owned by the National Trust, the area also includes the renowned Lydstep Caverns where the sea has carved fantastic shapes out of the cliffs. They are best seen at low tide.

Lydstep Point and caverns make a pleasant cliff-top walk from Tenby.

'Pont Werdd Cymru', Castellmartin, Penfro (Dyfed) Un o nodweddion amlycaf arfordir Penfro yw'r bwa hwn a naddwyd o'r calchfaen lleol gan y tywydd.

The Green Bridge of Wales, Castlemartin (Castellmartin), Pembrokeshire (Dyfed)
The Pembrokeshire Coast National Park has a coastline of unrivalled grandeur stretching from Cardigan in the north to Saundersfoot and Amroth in the south, and inland, the brooding Preseli Mountains to the east of Fishguard. Britain's smallest National Park, its chief glory is the truly wonderful cliff scenery which has an official long distance footpath following its seaward perimeter for much of the way, running to a total length of 167 miles.

This part of the Pembrokeshire coast is made of a carboniferous limestone and is part of the great saucer that includes the South Wales coalfields. Although hard, this sort of limestone is subject to erosion by the heavy seas that sweep in on the sou'westerly gales from the Atlantic. The result is a mass of grotesquely carved rocks and caves.

One of the most celebrated features is situated near Castlemartin, (on an Army firing range), and has the imaginative title of 'The Green Bridge of Wales'. Presumably, at some time in the future, this graceful arch will also be eroded by further weathering, and action by sea, to form an isolated stack — similar to the Elegug Stacks, nearby — a process which, in time values, renders Man's existence on Earth, quite irrelevant.

94

Palas Esgobol Llandyfâi, Penfro (Dyfed)
Adfeilion palas caerog i esgobion Tyddewi o'r
bedwaredd ganrif ar ddeg.

*Lamphey Palace (Llandyfai),
Pembrokeshire (Dyfed)* About one mile
east of Pembroke are situated the impressive ruins of Lamphey Palace, once part of
the Bishopric of St Davids. Now in the care
of The Department of the Environment, and
standing amongst well-tended lawns, this
medieval manor is very often associated
with Bishop Henry Gower (1327-47). A
feature is the arcaded parapets, found also
in the equally magnificent Bishop's Palace
at St Davids for which Bishop Gower was
also largely responsible. Lamphey Palace
chapel also has a splendid window of the
Perpendicular period, visible here on the
right.

A short distance from the Palace is
Lamphey village straddling the main road
from Pembroke to Tenby on a narrow tight
bend which swings around the local church.
A notable feature of this fine ecclesiastical
building is the unusually high tower, a
landmark for miles around.

Pentre Ifan, Mynydd Preseli, Penfro (Dyfed)
Credir mai hon yw'r gromlech berffeithiaf ym Mhrydain, a chysylltir hi â Stonehenge yn Lloegr a safleoedd cyn-hanes tebyg yn Iwerddon.

Pentre Ifan, Preseli Mountains (Mynydd Preseli), Pembrokeshire (Dyfed) In northern Pembrokeshire rise the smooth, but steep slopes of Mynydd Preseli — the Preseli Mountains. These mysterious hills have attracted legends and myths for centuries, and at Carnmenyn is an outcrop of the 'bluestones' that form the inner circle of Stonehenge in Wiltshire. They are believed to have been dragged to the Shores of Milford Haven then floated up the Bristol Channel and the Wiltshire Avon to the edge of Salisbury Plain. Equally impressive is the Megalithic chambered tomb known as *Pentre Ifan*, found on the northern slopes of the Preseli Mountains, within a maze of country lanes. Three uprights support a huge capstone, a feature which archaeologists have linked with similar sites in Ireland and the settlement of a wave of prehistoric Celtic invaders from Spain and Portugal.

Morglawdd Abergwaun, Penfro (Dyfed)
Gellir croesi i'r Iwerddon oddi yma, ac mae'r
harbwr bellach yn hafan i longwyr pleser.

Lower Fishguard (Abergwaun),
Pembrokeshire (Dyfed)   The main A40
road from London, if followed to its ultimate
destination, will bring the traveller to
Fishguard, on Pembrokeshire's northern
coast. The mainline railway from Padding-
ton also terminates at Fishguard, for
steamers to Rosslare in Southern Ireland.
Fishguard Bay is one of many similar bays in
the huge sweep of Cardigan Bay finishing at
Lleyn Peninsula in North Wales.

Sufficiently distant from the commercial
aspects of Fishguard, is Lower Fishguard, a
delightful cluster of old wharfs and
cottages, where the Gwaun River meets the
sea. The pier here was built by a celebrated
local character, Samuel Fenton, in the 18th
century to serve the pilchard fishermen who
fished the shoals then swarming round the
Welsh coast. The shoals ceased coming and
the trade died out. The harbour is now a
flourishing yacht haven.

Lower Fishguard was chosen for the tele-
vision film *Under Milkwood* by Dylan
Thomas, and starred fellow Welshman,
Richard Burton.

Porth-clais, Penfro (Dyfed) Yn ddiweddar atgyweiriwyd muriau'r harbwr a'r odynnau calch yn debyg i'r hyn oeddynt pan oedd gweithgarwch morwrol yr ardal yn ei anterth ddwy neu dair canrif yn ôl.

Porth-clais, Pembrokeshire (Dyfed)
Porth-clais was formerly the harbour for St David's. It is now used by pleasure craft, but previously it witnessed much seafaring activity, particularly during the 16th and 17th centuries, when corn, malt and wool arrived from Merioneth, Bristol and Barnstaple.

Recently, the harbour walls and lime kilns have been restored, and further contribute to a picturesque scene where the River Alun — which flows past St Davids Cathedral — reaches the sea.

Trwyncynddeiriog, Penfro (Dyfed) Bydd cerddwyr Llwybr Troed Arfordir Penfro yn siwr o werthfawrogi'r olygfa o'r clogwyni sy'n nodweddiadol o'r ardal.

Trwyncynddeiriog, Pembrokeshire (Dyfed)
To the ancient cartographer Ptolemy, this rocky promontary was Octapitarum the 'Eight Perils' — or the gates to the edge of the world and empty shoreless waters of infinite extent. Its name means 'point of fury'.

In 1978, John Merrill was the first person to walk the entire coastline of Great Britain, a journey of around 7,000 miles, and he would have tackled the 167-mile Pembrokeshire Coastal Footpath in brisk style.

The present scene, however, can be enjoyed in a much more leisurely fashion from the car-park at St Davids. Linked with Porth-clais and St Non's Chapel — the path well described in one of the National Parks many walking leaflets — will provide a memorable day for those walkers whose destination is no further than their parked car or hotel.

The cliff scenery encountered is typical of the area, and repeats itself over much of the peninsula in many fascinating variations, exploration of which, could well occupy an entire holiday.

Capel Non, Penfro (Dyfed) I'r de o Dyddewi
mae llwybr yr arfordir yn mynd heibio i'r capel
hwn, a ystyrir yn fan geni Dewi Sant.

St Non's Chapel, Pembrokeshire (Dyfed)
South of St David's, the coastal footpath
passes St Non's Chapel, reputed to be the
birthplace, in about 462AD, of St David. The
chapel is dedicated to his mother, Nonna
(St Non). According to legend, his birth took
place during a thunderstorm when a spring
also broke out a few yards away, and this is
reputed to have remarkable healing powers.
Today, the well over the spring is still to be
seen, with its healing waters pursuing their
more natural course past St Non's Chapel,
on their short journey to the sea.

106

*Palas yr Esgob ac Eglwys Gadeiriol Tyddewi,
Penfro (Dyfed)*   Dyma bentref sy'n ddinas am
fod iddo eglwys gadeiriol; yma y ceir allor a
chysegr Dewi Sant ac ochr yn ochr â'r eglwys
y saif adfeilion hen Balas yr Esgob.

*The Bishop's Palace and St David's
Cathedral St David's (Tŷddewi),
Pembrokeshire (Dyfed)*   St David's is by
virtue of its cathedral Britain's smallest city.
Built in a hollow out of sight of marauders,
the present building houses a precious
casket reputedly containing the bones of St
David. In recent years this theory was put
firmly to the test when pathologists
examined the casket. To the surprise of
some, they found that the casket contained
not the remains of one, but of two persons.
However, those historians who knew their
facts about St David also knew that he was
buried with his martyred friend St Justinian.
Furthermore, St Justinian was a person
over six feet tall, whilst St David was known
to be a comparatively short man. Both these
theories were confirmed by the pathologists
and the sealed casket can still be viewed
today in its honoured place in Trinity
Chapel, just to the rear of the high altar.

The viewpoint is from the highest
accessible vantage point open to the public
of the Bishop's Palace, with the view
stretching beyond to the 'city' of St David's.
The Bishop's Palace is a reminder of two
aspects of the life bishops enjoyed in the
Middle Ages. First is the sheer grandeur and
scale of the Palace — built in the last two
decades of the 13th century. The second is
the need for fortification as battlements,
curtain walls and the massive gatehouse all
proclaim. Its ruinous condition is said to
have begun when the last Bishop (c1548)
shipped off the lead roof to provide a dowry
for his five daughters.

108

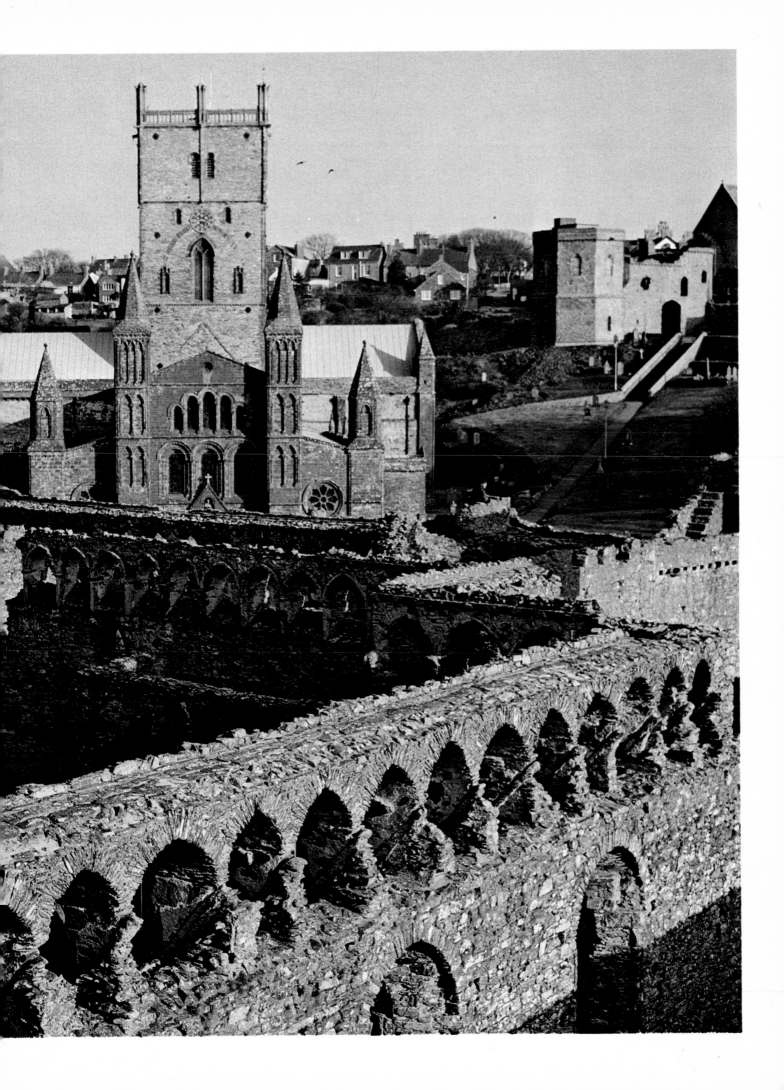

Golygfa fewnol. Eglwys Gadeiriol Tyddewi, Penfro (Dyfed) Tynnir sylw'r ymwelydd at y nenfwd gerfiedig foethus.

The interior of St David's Cathedral St David's (Tŷddewi), Pembrokeshire (Dyfed)
The first sight to capture the attention of a visitor to St David's Cathedral, is undoubtedly the unusual carved roof in Irish oak. Unusual, because this roof would seem more at home in an Arabian palace, than a sombre cathedral. Irish oak, because as Ireland is only 40 miles by sea, transportation of heavy materials in medieval times was, far easier by water than by land. The roof retained its light colour because of the salt in the atmosphere — the cathedral is no more than one mile from the sea in three directions.

The rood above the organ was added later and is made from the timbers of wrecked ships. It is said to weigh almost a ton.

List of Plates

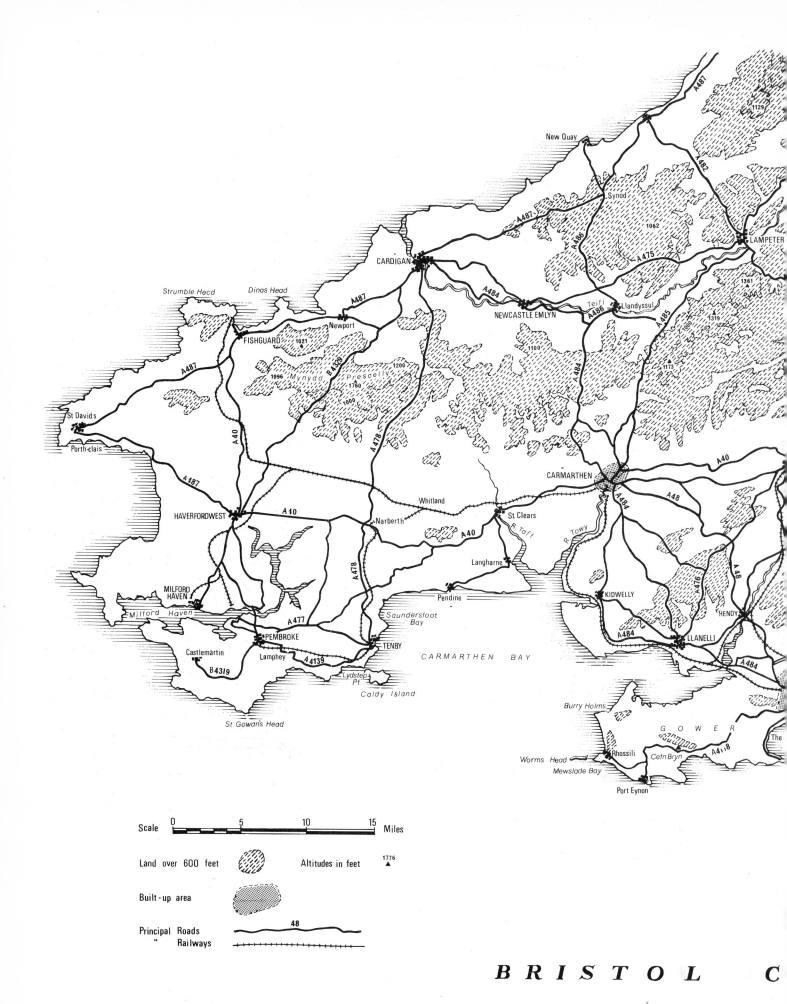

New Quay

LAMPETER

1129

A487

A482

Synod

1062

A487

A486

A475

1361

Teifi

A485

1319

CARDIGAN

Strumble Head

Dinas Head

A487

NEWCASTLE EMLYN

Llandyssul

1100

A484

A486

Newport

FISHGUARD

1021

1200

1173

A487

B4329

Mynydd Prescelly

1096

1760

1000

St Davids

1000

A40

A478

Porth-clais

A187

CARMARTHEN

A40

HAVERFORDWEST

A10

A48

Whitland

R. Towy

St Clears

A484

Narberth

A40

R Taff

A478

A476

A48

Langharne

MILFORD HAVEN

Milford Haven

A477

Kidwelly

HENDY

Saundersfoot
Bay

Pendine

A484

LLANELLI

PEMBROKE

TENBY

A484

Castlemartin

Lamphey

A4139

CARMARTHEN   BAY

Lydstep
Pt

B4319

Burry Holms

Caldy Island

G O W E R

St Gowan's Head

The

Rhossili

A4118

Cefn Bryn

Worms Head

Mewslade Bay

Port Eynon

Scale 0   5   10   15   Miles

Land over 600 feet   Altitudes in feet   1776 ▲

Built-up area

Principal Roads   48
    "   Railways

B R I S T O L   C

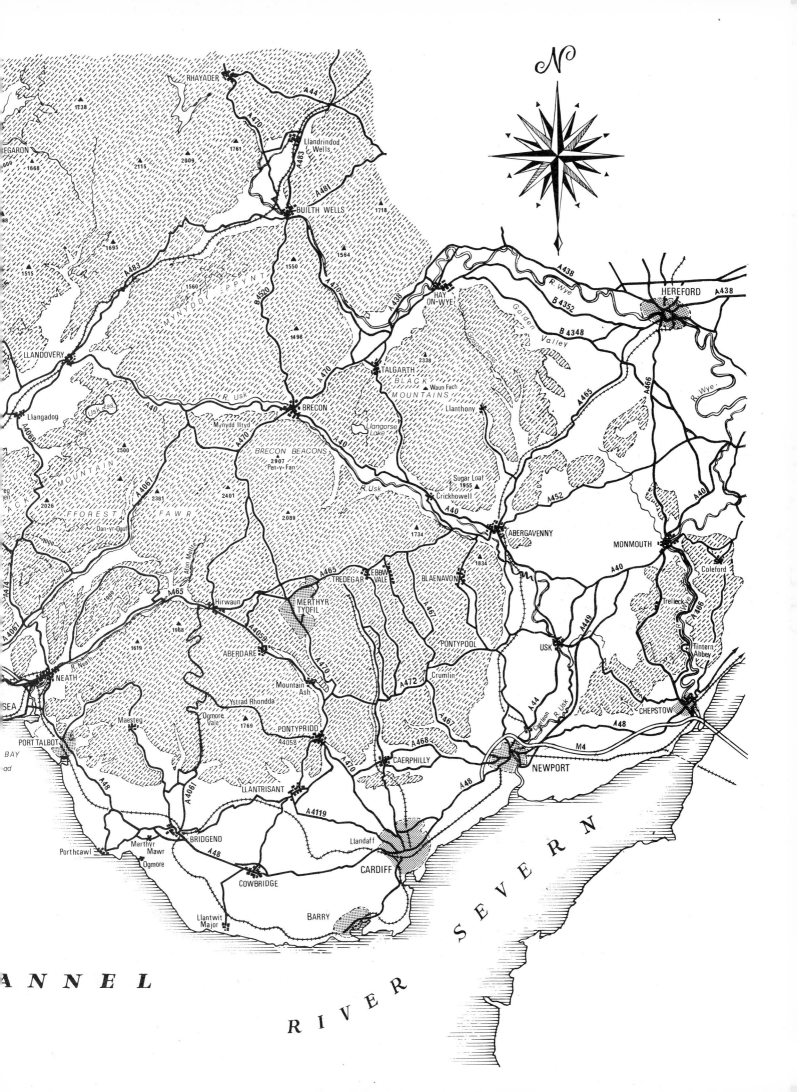

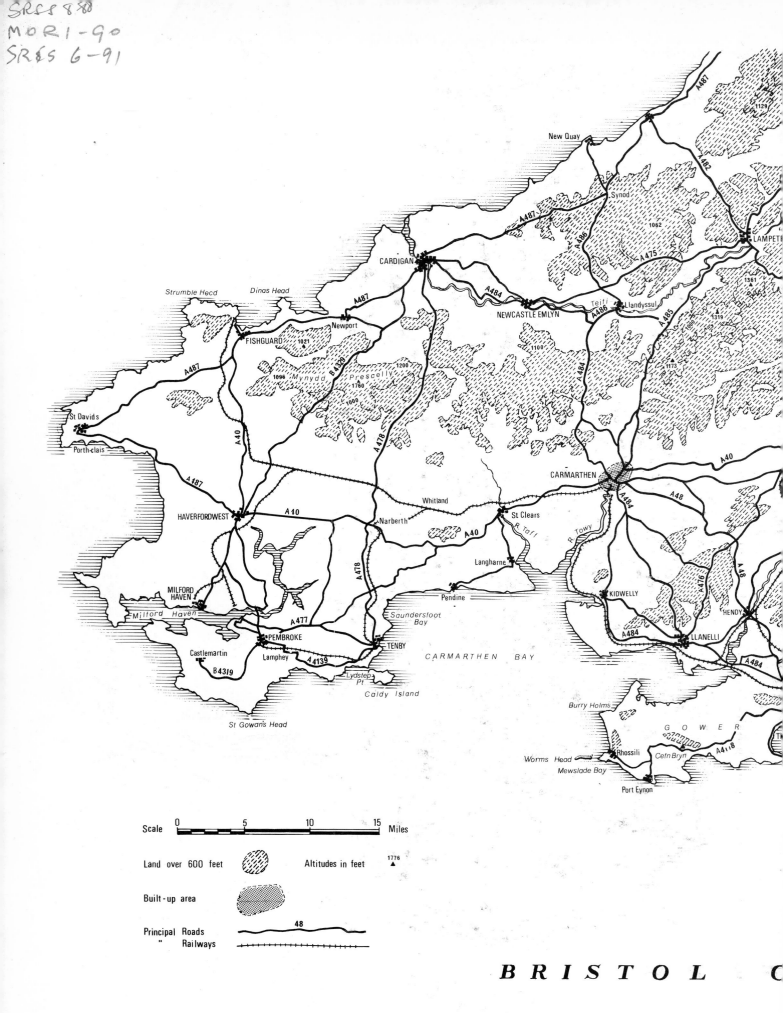

New Quay

Synod

1062

A487

A482

LAMPETI

A486

A475

CARDIGAN

A487

A484

Teifi

Llandyssul

1361

Strumble Head

Dinas Head

A486

NEWCASTLE EMLYN

A485

Newport

1021

1319

FISHGUARD

1096

Mynydd

B4329

Prescelly

1200

1100

1173

A487

1760

A484

1000

A478

A40

CARMARTHEN

A40

St Davids

A48

Porth-clais

A478

Whitland

A484

A187

St Clears

R Towy

HAVERFORDWEST

A40

Narberth

R Taf

A40

KIDWELLY

A476

A48

Langharne

A478

MILFORD
HAVEN

HENDY

Milford Haven

A477

Pendine

Saundersfoot
Bay

PEMBROKE

A484

Llanelli

Castlemartin

Lamphey

A4139

TENBY

A484

B4319

Lydstep
Pt

CARMARTHEN BAY

Caldy Island

Burry Holms

G O W E R

St Gowan's Head

Rhossili

Cefn Bryn

A4118

Worms Head

Mewslade Bay

Port Eynon

Scale 0   5   10   15 Miles

Land over 600 feet   Altitudes in feet   1776
                                                    ▲

Built-up area

Principal Roads
      "   Railways   48

B R I S T O L   C